GHOSTBUSTERS™

EERIE ERRORS & SUSPECT GHOSTS

Written by **Glenn Dakin**

Art by **John Ross**

Colors by **Alan Craddock**

Eaglemoss Ltd. 2020
1st Floor, Kensington Village, Avonmore Road
W14 8TS, London, UK. All rights reserved.

HOW TO USE THIS BOOK

What is a *Nerd Search*? It's a chance to nitpick your favorite stuff! We all adore discussing our top movies and TV shows. Be honest, we even love to find fault with them. Well, here we provide the faults! This is not your ordinary search-and-find book, but a diabolical test of your nerdular knowledge of your favorite topic. Instead of simply locating lost objects, you have to spot tiny errors no one but an obsessive superfan could spot.
Let us explain our categories…

NERD ALERT

Look out for **continuity errors** – things that just shouldn't be there. For example, it could be a character who wasn't in the scene, or a gadget that wasn't used at that point in time. In the Mr. Stay Puft-busting scene, for example, Janine should not be fighting alongside the guys – or the Library Ghost should not appear at all.

MOVIE MIX-UPS

These are **items or characters that are simply in the wrong movie**. If our featured scene is Slimer Showdown, from the first movie, then we should not see Dr. Janosz Poha from the sequel, cowering behind a table in the Sedgewick Hotel ballroom. Misplaced items can be anything from the Ecto-1 (before it was customized) to jars of mood slime or a stray spook.

MYTHS AND MANIFESTATIONS

To really test your ghostbusting credentials we've added **five 'out-of-universe' monsters, spooks or demons** into every spread. Simply spot if they are from the original *Ghostbusters* movies or not – and, for extra points, identify them! Our special feature on page 6 is there to help you.

SUPER QUIBBLES

There are just five of these in the entire book; they are **errors relating to behind-the-scenes information**, such as a character from a deleted scene appearing. Or maybe it is something planned for the movie that never made the final version. If you check out the scoring system below they will put you in reach of a score of biblical proportions, enabling you to hit a significant number…

SCORING SYSTEM

To enable you to judge between your friends who is the top Ghostbuster, we have a scoring system. Use your scorecard to keep track of your progress.

NERD ALERT: **5 points** each (five on each spread).

MOVIE MIX-UPS: **5 points** each (five on each spread).

MYTHS AND MANIFESTATIONS: **5 points** each – **2 points** for spotting and **3 points** if you know the name (five on each spread).

That's a maximum of **75 points** per spread. Across the eight spreads, that's a maximum of **600 points**. There are also just five **SUPER QUIBBLES** that appear in the book. If you spot ALL five, add **5,551,768 points** (that's **1,110,353.6** for each) to achieve the maximum total of **555-2368** – the Ghostbusters' original phone number! Check your result in the *How Did You Do?* section in the back of the book.

ANSWERS on page 24

WE'RE READY TO BELIEVE YOU...

Unless you have been living in a parallel dimension, you probably know a thing or two about *Ghostbusters*. But as a phenomenon, it may be more incredible than you even realize. How often in cinema does one movie create a whole genre? *Ghostbusters* is credited with inventing the blockbuster special effects comedy.

The first movie generated such fan interest that its ideas were subjected to more intense scrutiny than the average comedy would face. Was ectoplasm a thing? Could you really catch a ghost? If so, how could you hold an intangible being captive? The central concept alone was a nerd's feeding frenzy.

Interest in the characters provoked more issues. How come Venkman injected Dana with Thorazine, when he is a doctor of parapsychology and psychology, rather than medicine? Were Egon and Janine becoming an item? Also, mathematicians (and bakers) pointed out that Egon's famous 35 foot Twinkie would weigh a LOT more than 600 pounds… it would be closer to 50 tons! Now that's a big Twinkie…

SPONGE MIGRATION

Then there were those who studied the script more forensically… Was Gozer a real Ancient Sumerian deity? Can you really witness a mass sponge migration? Why did Ray refer to the Tunguska blast as being in 1909, when lovers of weird phenomena know it famously occurred in 1908? Did Ray know of ANOTHER Tunguska event?

Also, devotees of the original film watched the second movie like hawks for changes in ghostbusting gear, mythology and jargon. Questions were raised, like how come the team in the movie have the real life *Ghostbusters* theme song? Just how did a supernatural elimination business end up with a theme song written and performed by Ray Parker, Jr.?

There was much more to puzzle over. Why did the operation of the ghost trap change – do you have to tread on the control pedal once, twice, or keep your foot down throughout? How could Vigo have taken over the world if he was reborn as a baby? Was Janine given a quirky makeover so she resembled her cartoon character more? And how could anyone in New York possibly have not believed that the Ghostbusters were real after the events of the first movie?

The two movies inspired endless discussions among fans. This *Nerd Search* taps into that enthusiasm and gives you a chance to show you are as smart as Egon and have a depth of knowledge the equivalent of *Tobin's Spirit Guide*. If you think you're the biggest *Ghostbusters* fan in the world, then this book actually allows you to prove it. We're ready to believe you!

MYTHS AND MANIFESTATIONS...
And How To Spot Them

Do you believe in UFOs, astral projections, the Loch Ness Monster and the theory of Atlantis? If the answer is yes, then not only are you qualified to work for Ghostbusters, but you should also be pretty well up on your knowledge of supernatural beings. That's going to help you score big in the world of *Nerd Search*.

To add an extra dimension to this book, we are asking you to spot spooks, monsters and mythical menaces that do not specifically belong to the *Ghostbusters* movies. As the films themselves draw on a wide variety of supernatural phenomena, so too do the scary monsters in this unique artworks.

The big baddie in the first movie, Gozer the Gozerian, is supposedly a deity of the ancient Sumerians and Mesopotamians, from around 6000 BC. We have also drawn on ancient myth for some of our menaces. Many of the Greek gods and monsters featured have been made famous by movie appearances and entered into popular consciousness, like Hades, god of the Underworld, and creatures like Medusa, the Minotaur and the Sirens.

Ancient Egyptian myth gives us Anubis, the jackal-headed god of the dead, and a similar figure occurs, but in female form, in the shape of Hel, from Norse tales.

FIENDS OF FOLKLORE

The Terror Dogs that work for Gozer in the first movie are typical of demonic dogs that occur in many cultures. Greece has Cerberus, the three-headed dog that guards the way to the Underworld, and England has its own demon dog, Black Shuck, the sight of which usually portends death.

Demon dogs are joined in this book by other creatures from folklore like dragons and the griffin. More human monsters like the werewolf, ogres and trolls derive from European and, more specifically, Scandinavian folklore. Canada and the snowy wastes of North America have their own flesh-eating Wendigo.

The animated company mascot, the Stay Puft Marshmallow Man, could be seen as a type of golem, a man-like being of Jewish folklore, conjured to life from clay (or in this case, sugar and gelatin). We have a creature of this type for you to spot.

Most fans recall the Zombie Taxi Driver from the first movie – and may well have encountered him on a trip to New York! Other similar undead dudes are among our invaders, including a Chinese hopping zombie called a jiangshi (with characteristic pigtail) and traditional voodoo zombies. We also have a generic, reanimated corpse zombie – the typical version familiar from movies and comic-books.

HEADLESS HORRORS

A tragic historic event, the fate of the RMS *Titanic*, inspires a ghostly return in *Ghostbusters II*. Tragic historic spooks also form part of our gang of intruders, including Henry VIII's second wife Anne Boleyn, who was beheaded. Also, we have the spirit of Mary, Queen of Scots, who suffered a similar fate.

Another type of spook is the stuff of today's urban myth, like the Ghostly Jogger Peter catches at Central Park. We feature another ghost of the modern highway – don't give them a lift!

Slimer is probably the most popular specter from the *Ghostbusters* movies. Endlessly greedy, he is reminiscent of the hungry ghosts of China. China also provides the hanged ghosts, whose strangled look with tongue sticking out betrays the manner of death. Also from the East, Japan gives us tales of manekute no yurei – ghostly spirits that sometimes manifest as beckoning hands.

Vigo the Carpathian from *Ghostbusters II* is a mortal sorcerer, whose legend was based on the tales of Vlad the Impaler, ruler of Wallachia in the 15th century. The story of Count Dracula was also inspired by Vlad. Dracula was distilled from vampiric legend by author Bram Stoker (in 1897) and we have a couple of other such fictional fiends in our ranks.

SCREAMING SKULLS

The Library Ghost at the start of the first movie is typical of the spooky female apparition common worldwide. There are many tales of a 'white lady' or 'gray lady' ghost. Other creepy figures are the ghostly monks and phantom pipers that haunt castles and other historic sites.

Not all weird phenomena fall into the same categories. In *Ghostbusters II* we have a ghostly painting. Inanimate objects have frequently been suspected of having supernatural qualities, like so-called screaming skulls, several of which are said to exist in Europe. On a grander scale, ghost trains have been the stuff of tales for many years, and we have provided a well-documented ghost ship.

This mini spirit-guide should set you up for a spot of ghost-hunting yourself.
Bust those spooks and monsters and save us from forty years of darkness…
or at least a little mass hysteria.

THE LIBRARY LURKER

This is big… this is very big. There's a full torso apparition in the New York Public Library basement, and she doesn't like Ray's suggestion that the team 'get her!'

MYTHS & MANIFESTATIONS

The scene has been invaded by FIVE SUSPECT GHOSTS, CREEPY PHENOMENA that were not in the original *Ghostbusters* movies. Can you spot the intruders and name them? Think Oriental and Mexican among others…

NERD ALERT

The suspect ghosts have added eerie errors across this whole book! There are FIVE SERIOUS CONTINUITY ERRORS in this image! They could be characters in the wrong scene, costume errors or gadget glitches. **Nail them, now!**

MOVIE MIX-UPS

FIVE ITEMS from the second movie are lurking in this classic scene. Can you find them and stop this distortion of the fabric of reality?

SLIMER SHOWDOWN

He's an ugly little spud and he's already slimed Venkman.
Everyone's favorite full-roaming vapor needs taking down.
The Sedgewick Hotel ballroom may not survive the process…

NERD ALERT

Weird things happen on the
12th Floor, like movie continuity
falling apart. THE MISTAKES HERE
are of many kinds; they could be
**sequential, conceptual or things
that are just plain wrong…**

MYTHS & MANIFESTATIONS

FIVE MORE FOOTLOOSE PHENOMENA
from the wide world of general creepiness
are enjoying the ballroom entertainment.
Can you spot the weirdness
that is not *Ghostbusters*-related?
Think Transylvania and Japan
for starters…

MOVIE MIX-UPS

MORE ITEMS from
Ghostbusters II have joined
the party. Bust them before
they bust our sense
of reality!

ECTO EXPLOSION

Keep running! Walter Peck has shut down the Ecto Containment system – which Egon says would be like dropping a bomb in the city. The liberated ghosts are now free to wreak havoc.

NERD ALERT

The suspect ghosts have added **FIVE SERIOUS CONTINUITY-RELATED ANOMALIES** to this scene. They could be characters who were not in the movie at this point, or mere wardrobe weirdness. How about prop problems? **Get busting!**

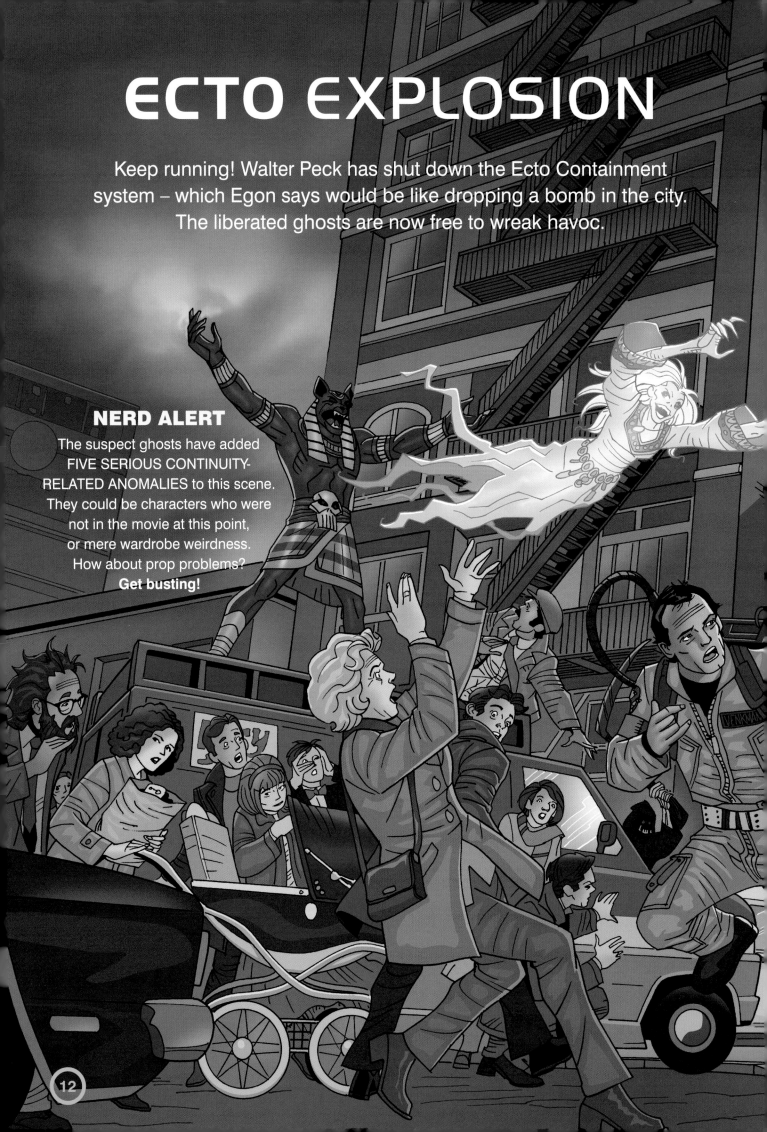

MYTHS & MANIFESTATIONS

Those creepy intruders are back.
FIVE OF THE SPOOKS, CREATURES
OR MYTHICAL MARAUDERS are
not from the *Ghostbusters* movies.
Name and shame them.
Think Irish and Egyptian,
among others…

MOVIE MIX-UPS

Get your Ecto goggles on!
STUFF FROM THE SECOND
MOVIE has been added to
the mayhem in this
classic scene!

HOOK & LADDER

MARSHMALLOW MELTDOWN

This is extraordinarily bad. The guys were commanded by Gozer to choose the form of the Destructor, and Ray, seeking refuge in safe memories, came up with the Stay Puft Marshmallow Man…

MYTHS & MANIFESTATIONS

Monstrous visitations haunt the city – can you SPOT THE FIVE that shouldn't be in the movie? This time, there are a couple of movie-star manifestations in there!

NERD ALERT

As if a towering, demonic marshmallow wasn't bad enough, there are FIVE CONTINUITY CATASTROPHES here. **Find them – or are you terrified beyond the capacity for rational thought?**

MOVIE MIX-UPS

FIVE MORE ITEMS from the sequel are hidden in this scene. **Can you spot them?** Don't worry if you can't – there's definitely a slim chance that reality will survive.

COURTROOM CHAOS

The court may not recognize the existence of ghosts,
but Judge Wexler sure has to put up with some malarkey
from the Scoleri Brothers… who he once sent to the chair!

MYTHS & MANIFESTATIONS

FIVE MORE WEIRD CREATURES of myth,
legend, folklore and superstition have
turned up to witness the proceedings!
We have folkloric and ancient Greek
menaces, among many more!

NERD ALERT

There are some HIGHLY
IRREGULAR CONTRAVENTIONS
OF CONTINUITY in this scene.
**Find them before the judge
has us all burnt at the stake!**

MOVIE MIX-UPS

Now you're looking for INVASIVE ITEMS AND CHARACTERS from the first movie. Show you are a good judge by spotting them among the madness here…

17

TRANSIT TERROR

There could never be a better time to go down into the old abandoned transit system. There's a river of slime to discover and possibly a surge in the cockroach population...

MYTHS & MANIFESTATIONS

The transit tunnels are a perfect hang-out for some of the CREEPIEST GENERIC AND HISTORIC SPOOKS around. One is of Chinese origin, and another of these dudes spent his whole life in a very similar haunt...

MOVIE MIX-UPS

Lurking in the darkness are FIVE MORE ELEMENTS from the first movie. Find them before the *City of Albany* steams over you, too.

NERD ALERT

Trains don't always run on time – but this one is 50 years too late. **Can you spot FIVE CONTINUITY GLITCHES that are just as weird?**

STATUE SMACKDOWN

Midnight on New Year's Eve in New York City and Lady Liberty – powered by the Ghostbusters and positive mood slime – is ready to bring the hammer down! Will the future belong to Vigo or mere mortals?

NERD ALERT

MOVIE MISTAKES, can we learn to love them? Sure, like Dana can learn to love Janosz in Vigo's new order! **So pull out your blooper blasters and let's cook!**

MOVIE MIX-UPS

Hidden in this scene are FIVE MORE SNEAKY INSERTS from the original movie. It's time to erase those errors, be they vehicular or spook-tacular.

MYTHS & MANIFESTATIONS

There's a creepy new urban myth ghost among the CLASSIC CREEPS AND HISTORIC HAUNTERS who have crashed this crazy New Year's Eve party! There's also a major Greek god and even a haunted ship... **Find them and name any you know!**

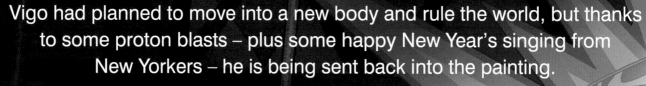

VENGEANCE ON VIGO

Vigo had planned to move into a new body and rule the world, but thanks to some proton blasts – plus some happy New Year's singing from New Yorkers – he is being sent back into the painting.

MYTHS & MANIFESTATIONS

Spot our LAST SELECTION OF SPOOKS, AND MONSTERS that do not belong in the *Ghostbusters* movies, and end their threat! Think historic, Nordic and North American!

REPENT! FOR THE END IS NEAR

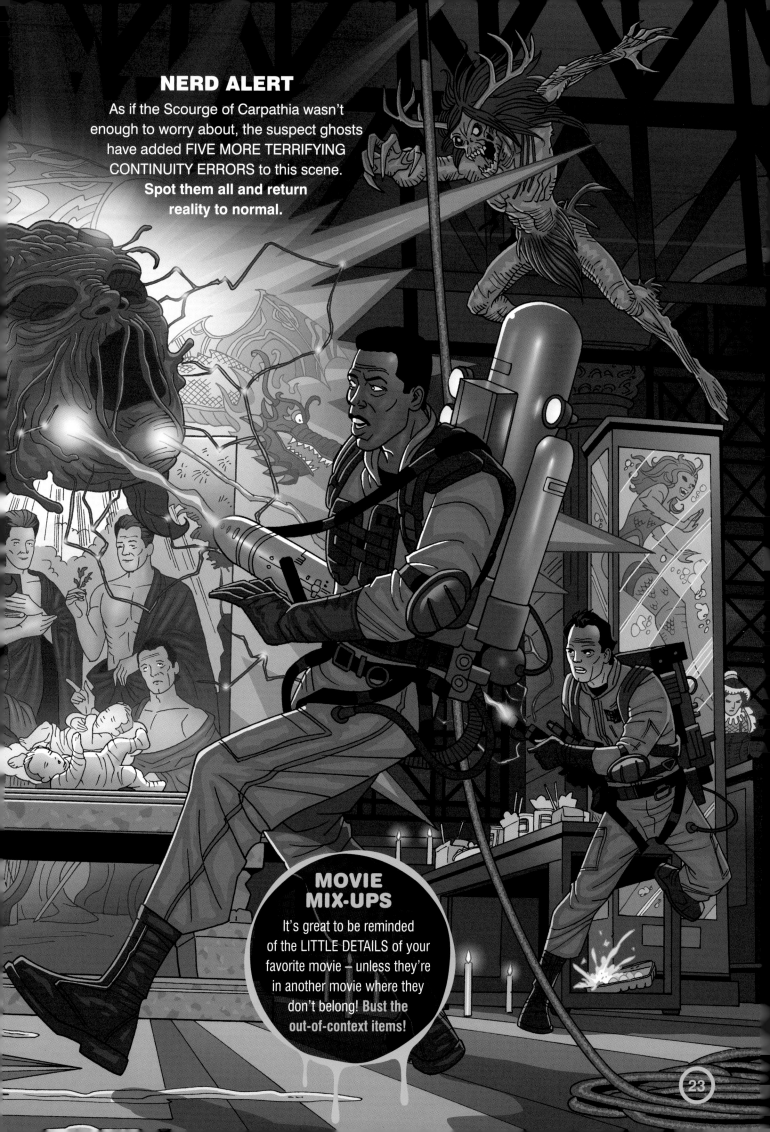

NERD ALERT

As if the Scourge of Carpathia wasn't enough to worry about, the suspect ghosts have added FIVE MORE TERRIFYING CONTINUITY ERRORS to this scene. **Spot them all and return reality to normal.**

MOVIE MIX-UPS

It's great to be reminded of the LITTLE DETAILS of your favorite movie – unless they're in another movie where they don't belong! Bust the out-of-context items!

THE LIBRARY LURKER

NERD ALERT
FIVE CONTINUITY ERRORS

1. C5. Winston is with the team – wrong, he had not joined yet! In fact, the Ghostbusters organization itself didn't actually exist at this point.

2. D5. Venkman is dressed as he appears in the Ghostbusters TV advert.

3. C6. Egon has his earphones on. He was using them earlier, in the library reading room, but lowered them after being pranked by Venkman.

4. E2. The library administrator does not go to the basement. In fact, he would have had to cross a continent to do so, as the upstairs library scenes were filmed in New York, but the basement scene was filmed in Los Angeles Central Library!

5. E6. The stack of books was seen elsewhere in the basement, before the ghost turns ugly!

MOVIE MIX-UPS
Items from *Ghostbusters II*

6. E7. The tape player is from the kids' party scene.

7. D2. The 'Occult Books' display is from Ray's shop.

8. E7. Did you recognize the Ghostly Jogger who is captured running round Central Park?

9. E3. Polarity rectification tripod, as used in Orrefors up-market glass store.

10. E5. Ghostbusters hot beverage thermal mug – with free balloon for the kids – as seen in their TV advert!

MYTHS AND MANIFESTATIONS

11. B2. Did you spot the golem? These stone or clay men are animated by magic.

12. E7. This spooky cat mummy is from ancient Egypt.

13. E3. Mexican Day of the Dead spirit.

14. C6. Everyone's favorite howler, the cuddly werewolf.

15. E3. Chinese hopping zombie, sometimes vampiric, in typical Qing Dynasty official's uniform.

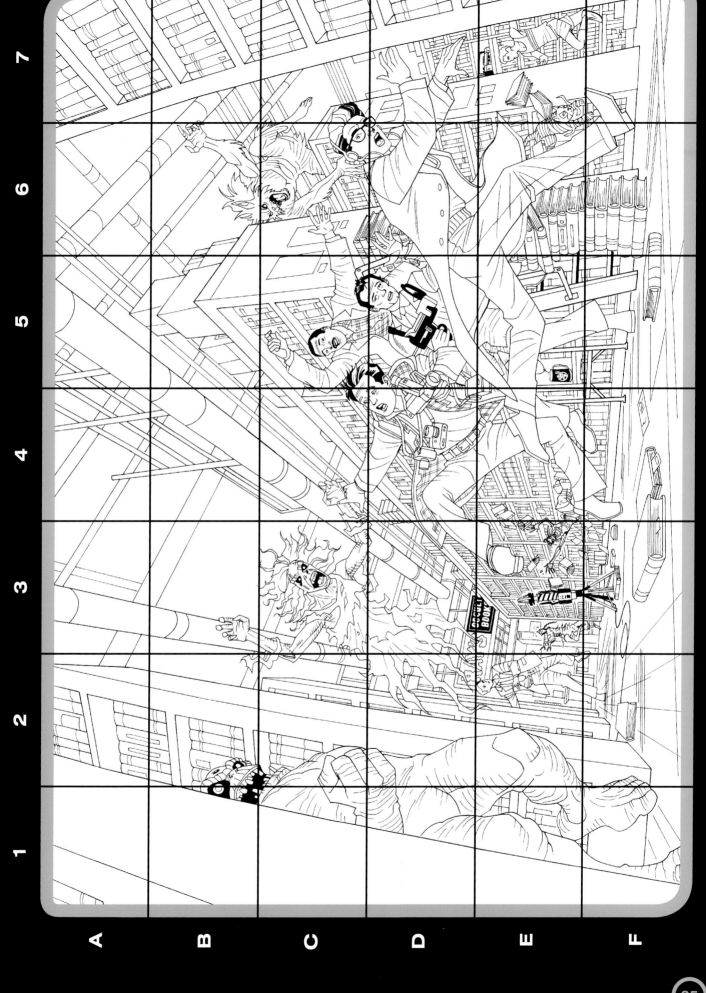

SLIMER SHOWDOWN

NERD ALERT
FIVE CONTINUITY ERRORS

1. C3. Ray should be wearing the Ecto Goggles, not Peter.

2. C2. The hotel manager does not enter the Alhambra Ballroom during the bust.

3. C4. The guys do NOT cross the streams! Not here, anyway. Some fans will know this scene is actually where the danger of crossing the streams is first mentioned. But the scene was actually shot after the showdown with Stay Puft. It was during that scene that the idea of crossing the streams was improvised by the cast on the spot. Then the dialogue introducing the idea was inserted into this scene to set up the climax later.

4. C5. Slimer should not have any legs. He's a Class 5 full-roaming vapor. In fact, he did have legs when performed as a foam-rubber puppet by Mark Wilson, but the legs were hidden by black velvet.

5. D3. The Sedgewick Hotel ballroom sign should not be in the room. It was outside.

MOVIE MIX-UPS
Items From *Ghostbusters II*

6. C6. Painting of Vigo.

7. E1. Ray picks up this soft toy in Dana's baby's room.

8. C6. Egon wears this helmet when the team are digging up First Avenue in the sequel.

9. D1. Jar of mood slime, as seen on the evidence desk in the courtroom scene.

10. C6. Egon's lab assistant was never in the first movie!

MYTHS AND MANIFESTATIONS

11. F7. Ghostly hands, sometimes beckoning or seeking attention appear in many cultures, including Japan.

12. C1. Pray you don't run into a ghost monk, like this one. Many have been seen haunting castles and religious sites across the UK.

13. C7. Count me in! Dracula himself invites you to a glass of something red...

14. D6. He's a scream – the screaming skull is a spooky tradition, mainly in England.

15. E5. Black dogs, demon dogs and hell-hounds are harbingers of doom, sighted in folklore across Europe. These guys don't play 'fetch,' unless they've come to fetch you!

Super Quibble 1: C7. Did you spot the Onionhead Ghost in the scene?

This isn't a character from the movies, or a real-life phenomenon. Top nerds will know that when Slimer was first invented, he was called the Onionhead Ghost by the crew working on the picture. Not because he looked like an onion, by the way, but because he stank! Bonus points if this smelly spook set your P.K.E. meter off!

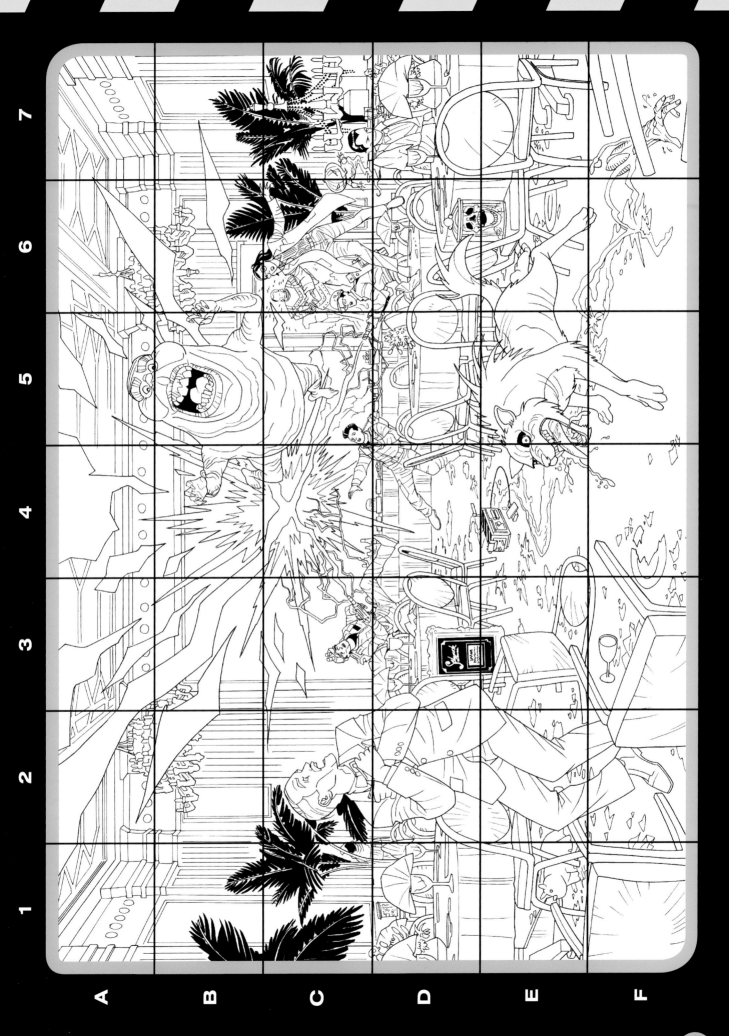

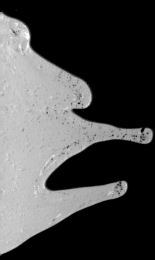

ECTO EXPLOSION

NERD ALERT
FIVE CONTINUITY ERRORS

1. D3. Wrong outfit again! Venkman is not in ghostbusting gear when Walter Peck triggers the Ecto-Containment Unit meltdown.

2. E5. Ray should not be running out of the HQ. He isn't there at this time.

3. E5. The Ghostbusters sign is flipped the wrong way on the building.

4. E4. Ecto-1 is parked outside... wrong – it hadn't arrived yet, and had to park outside police barriers.

5. E5. Tully shouldn't be wearing the brainwave-scanning helmet; it was taken off earlier. Also, our artist has thrown in an extra, just-for-fun error. Did you know that the window of the HQ did not explode outwards during the ecto explosion?

MOVIE MIX-UPS
Items From *Ghostbusters II*

6. E4. Ray is wearing a clown hat from the kids' party scene.

D1. Dana is passing by with her pram. She wasn't there and the baby wasn't born yet! Did you know that in an early version of the script, Dana wasn't in the movie at all. The mother in the film was a different character called Lane – and Vigo, a long-lived mystic in the guise of a musician, was the baby's real father!

7. E5. Janine shouldn't be wearing this eye-catching fake fur and slime-green gloves – she wears these in the second movie when inviting Tully to babysit with her.

8. A6. Emerging from the building's roof is the Cinema Ghost. Wrong movie! This appears after the river of psychomagnotheric slime triggers supernatural manifestations!

9. C7. Don't tell me you didn't spot Lady Liberty strolling by.

MYTHS AND MANIFESTATIONS

10. E3. The Grim Reaper, Death in person, makes an appearance. He has been dying to get in!

11. C6. A Griffin – lion body, eagle beak and wings. These creatures – symbols of divine power – have been reported in legend since ancient Egyptian, Greek and Roman times.

12. C2. Anubis, the ancient Egyptian God of the Dead.

13. C3. A wailing banshee of Irish legend. Its sad cry is said to foreshadow tragedy to those that hear it.

14. E4. Generic zombie. Not to be confused with the Zombie Taxi Driver who enters a cab via its exhaust pipe and manifests as a decomposing corpse in the first movie!

Super Quibble 2: C4. If you knew the word Gozer should not appear on the wall, the bonus points are yours. Fans who have investigated behind-the-scenes will know that Dan Aykroyd took the word 'Gozer' from graffiti said to appear in a true-life poltergeist incident. That graffiti is part of the movie's story but never appeared on screen.

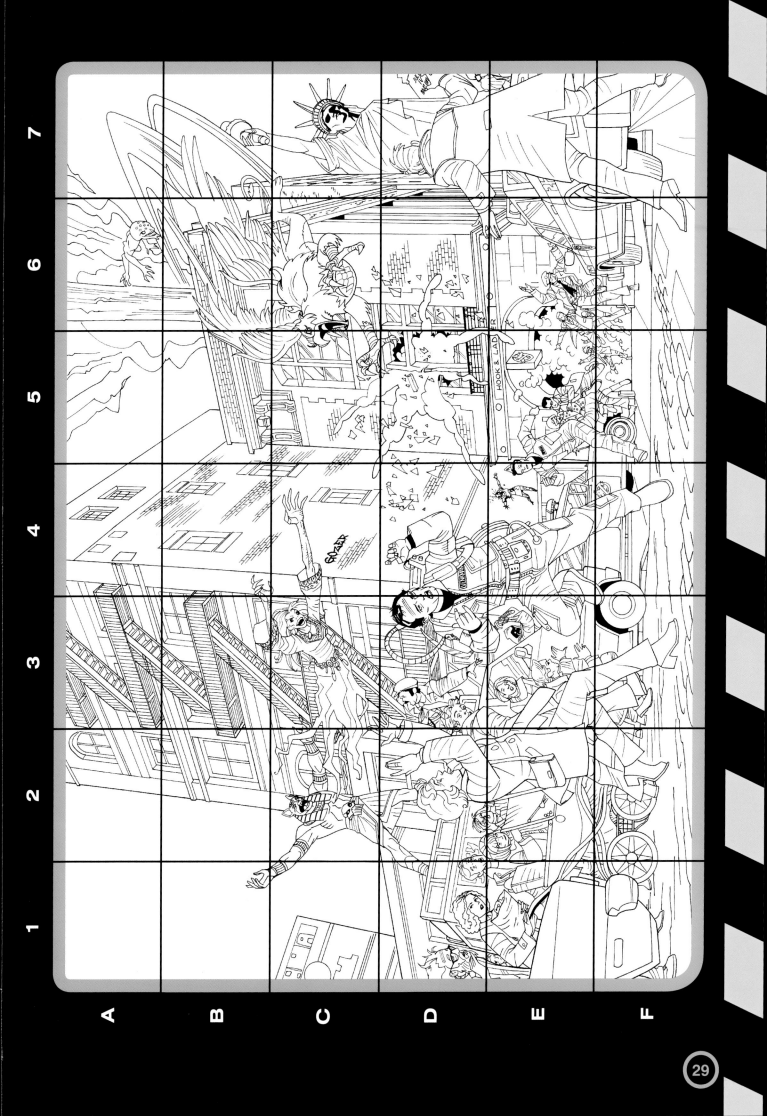

MARSHMALLOW MELTDOWN

NERD ALERT
FIVE CONTINUITY ERRORS

1. C3. The Stay Puft Marshmallow Man should not have fangs! The whole gag was that he actually looked harmless. He was originally created as a combination of the Michelin Man and the Pillsbury Doughboy.

2. C5. Egon should not be holding a P.K.E. meter. He uses a proton gun with the others.

3. C5. Ray should not have marshmallow on him, as they haven't busted Stay Puft yet! It was really shaving foam, anyway.

4. F3. There should not be a ghost trap – these are never used in the big showdown.

5. D7. Dana in her possessed-by-Zuul-state should not be there – she had turned into a dog by now!

MOVIE MIX-UPS
Items from *Ghostbusters II*

6. D7. Dana's baby should not be in the scene!

7. C2. Did you spot the phantom nanny? Janosz was never in the first movie.

8. E1. The ghost train from the abandoned pneumatic transit line is in the distance.

9. B6. Tully, as a Ghostbuster, does not appear in this scene. He was also transformed into a supernatural beast, like Dana.

10. C5. Venkman wears a Santa hat in the second movie ghostbusting montage, not in the first!

MYTHS AND MANIFESTATIONS

11. C7. Frankenstein's monster, invented by novelist Mary Shelley for her 1818 novel. A ghoulish creature constructed from parts of dead bodies, the infamous character has featured many times on the big screen.

12. E3. The mummy! Many ancient civilizations, including the Egyptians, mummified their dead, and apparently some didn't stay dead!

13. A6. White lady ghost – these appear in many cultures as tragic figures, or portents of doom, or both!

14. E3. Cerberus, the three-headed dog, is guardian of the Underworld in Greek myth.

15. A7. Ghostly pipers are said to haunt many a Scottish castle. If you hear a weird moaning, don't worry – it probably isn't a ghost. Bagpipes just sound like that, anyway…

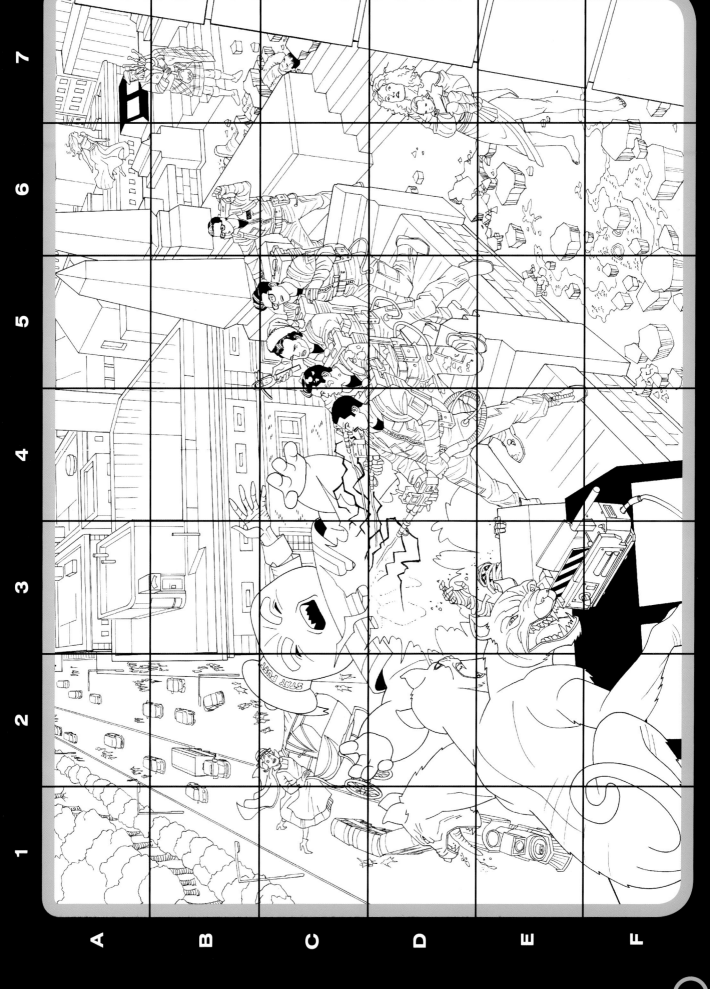

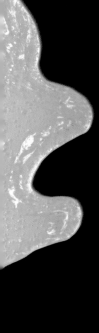

COURTROOM CHAOS

NERD ALERT
FIVE CONTINUITY ERRORS

1. C2. Judge Wexler should not be in his chair when the Scoleri Brothers are on the rampage. He had run for cover.

2. C5. Ray should not be tangling the bigger spook in his proton stream. Peter Venkman shows his skills in doing that!

3. C3. The other ghost ain't no Scoleri brother; that's the ghost from the Ghostbusters TV ad!

4. D2. How can the Ghostbusters gear still be on the table when it's also on their backs?

5. E1. There should be no panicking public in the room. All spectators had fled by now!

MOVIE MIX-UPS
Items from *Ghostbusters*

6. E7. You don't need telepathy to detect one of Venkman's Zener cards on the floor.

7. D5. This packet of Stay Puft marshmallows was seen in Dana's kitchen in the first movie.

8. C4. The city map showing supernatural activity is from the mayor's office.

9. C7. Did you recognize the video games from the firehouse in the first movie?

10. C1. That impressive plant is from the Sedgewick Hotel and there was one right outside the ballroom where Slimer was busted.

MYTHS AND MANIFESTATIONS

11. C3. A voodoo zombie. Before movies and horror comics took over the styling of zombies, their roots were in ancient voodoo rituals.

12. B5. Vampire in bat form. Vampires are said to be shape-shifters and are particularly at home 'hanging out' in bat form.

13. C2. Ogres have shared the world with us for centuries, according to some historical records. Not great news, as it seems they have a taste for human flesh.

14. B7. Everyone should have recognized Medusa, the gorgon of Greek myth. The snake hair and frosty looks are a giveaway.

15. D6. Here's a tough one to recognize, but not hard to know it wasn't in the *Ghostbusters* movies. A Chinese hanged ghost has popping out eyes and its tongue poking out!

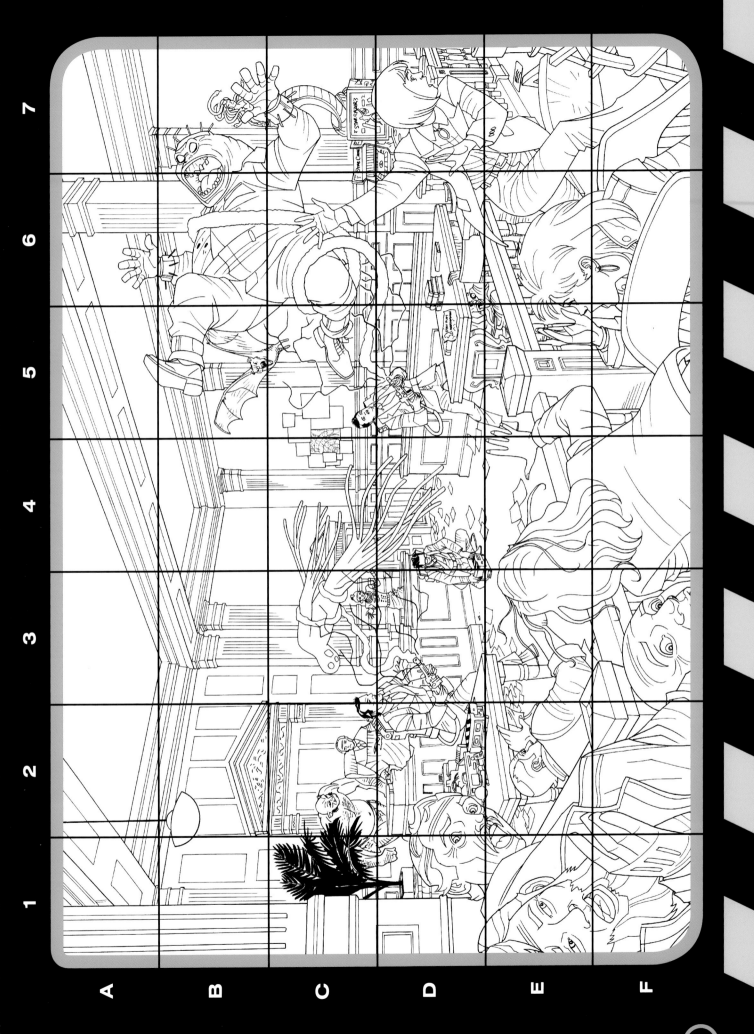

TRANSIT TERROR

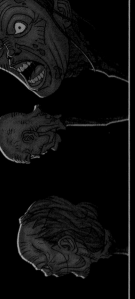

NERD ALERT
FIVE CONTINUITY ERRORS

1. D3-5. Only Winston is on the transit line when the train comes through.

2. C6. Venkman does not go on this adventure at all; he is having dinner with Dana.

3. D3. Winston should be carrying a spade, not a garden fork!

4. E5. The psychomagnotheric slime does not appear in the same scene as the ghost train. It's in a neighboring tunnel.

5. E1. The impaled heads are not there at the same time as the train.

MOVIE MIX-UPS
Items from *Ghostbusters*

6. C7. The Library Ghost, sometimes known as the Gray Lady, should not be in *Ghostbusters II*! Did you know her name is Eleanor Twitty?

7. C4. This red box on the wall is not part of the old transit equipment. It's the Ecto-Containment Unit, as seen in the first movie.

8. B1. The transit line is certainly not on the 22nd floor of the Shandor Building (Dana's apartment).

9. B7. This Terror Dog sculpture is from the roof of the same building.

10. C3. The Subway Ghost appears after the Ecto-Containment Unit explodes, when Walter Peck shuts it down.

MYTHS AND MANIFESTATIONS

11. C1. The dragon, in its typical European form – fire-breathing, winged, scaly and taloned.

12. E2. A Chinese hungry ghost. Spirits are consumed by terrible hunger as a punishment for not being generous in life.

13. C2. Anne Boleyn, the second wife of Henry VIII, was beheaded on his orders, and her headless ghost haunts many places – including the Tower of London and the New York Pneumatic Railway, apparently!

14. A6. Trolls come from Nordic folklore. They like lonely mountains or hiding under bridges, so this one fits in quite well here…

15. C5. You ought to recognize the Minotaur, a labyrinth dweller also at home here!

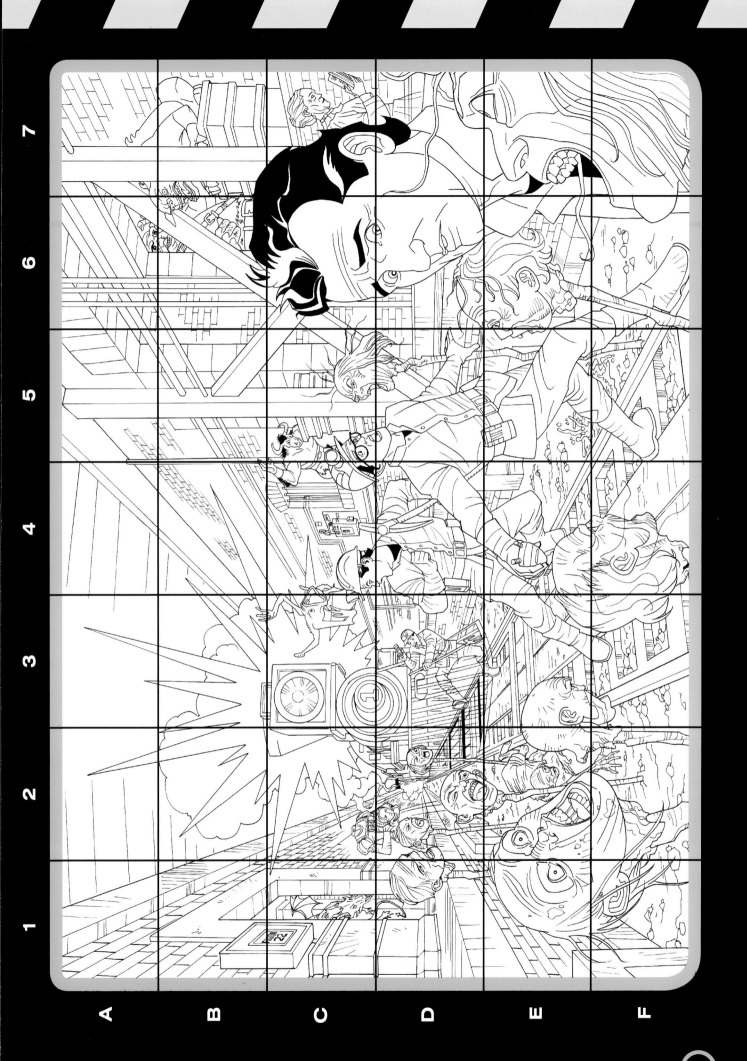

STATUE SMACKDOWN

NERD ALERT
FIVE CONTINUITY ERRORS

1. B5. The museum should be completely covered in slime.

2. D5-6. Ray and Winston cannot be in the foreground when they are inside the head of the Statue of Liberty!

3. A6. Lady Liberty is the wrong color. At this point in the movie she is reflecting the maroon glow of the slime.

4. B6. The hand with the torch should be striking the museum.

5. B1. The trees should not be in leaf, as this scene takes place on a wintry New Year's Eve.

MOVIE MIX-UPS
Items from *Ghostbusters*

6. E7. Did you spot the 1959 Cadillac Miller-Meteor in the scene? This is how it looks before it is turned into Ecto-1.

7. D5. The Lincoln Center fountain where Peter meets Dana should not be in front of the Museum of Art.

8. C1. The horse Louis Tully speaks to when he is possessed by Vinz Clortho. And no, the horse wasn't the gatekeeper!

9. D2. The Zombie Taxi Driver who appears after the big ectoplasm escape at the Ghostbusters HQ.

10. E5. This sinking cop car is from the big showdown scene at the Shandor Building.

MYTHS AND MANIFESTATIONS

10. D5. There are many headless horsemen in myth, frequently searching for their heads! Pictured here is the one from the Washington Irving tale, *The Legend of Sleepy Hollow*.

11. C3. Hades is the god of the Underworld, in Greek myth.

12. C5. There are ghosts and there are witches, and there are ghost witches! Doubly diabolical, they appear in murky photos, folklore and urban myth.

13. D7. The *Flying Dutchman* is a legendary ghost ship, doomed to sail the seas forever! Sightings stem from the late 18th Century.

14. D4. The phantom hitchhiker is a relatively modern urban myth, involving a hitchhiker who, once having secured a lift, vanishes!

Super Quibble 3: D1. Did you spot the two tramps looking on? In the original script, Bill Murray and Dan Aykroyd were going to dress up as hobos and comment on events. This idea was dropped for the final version, as it might just confuse viewers! Top marks if you knew about this behind-the-scenes stuff!

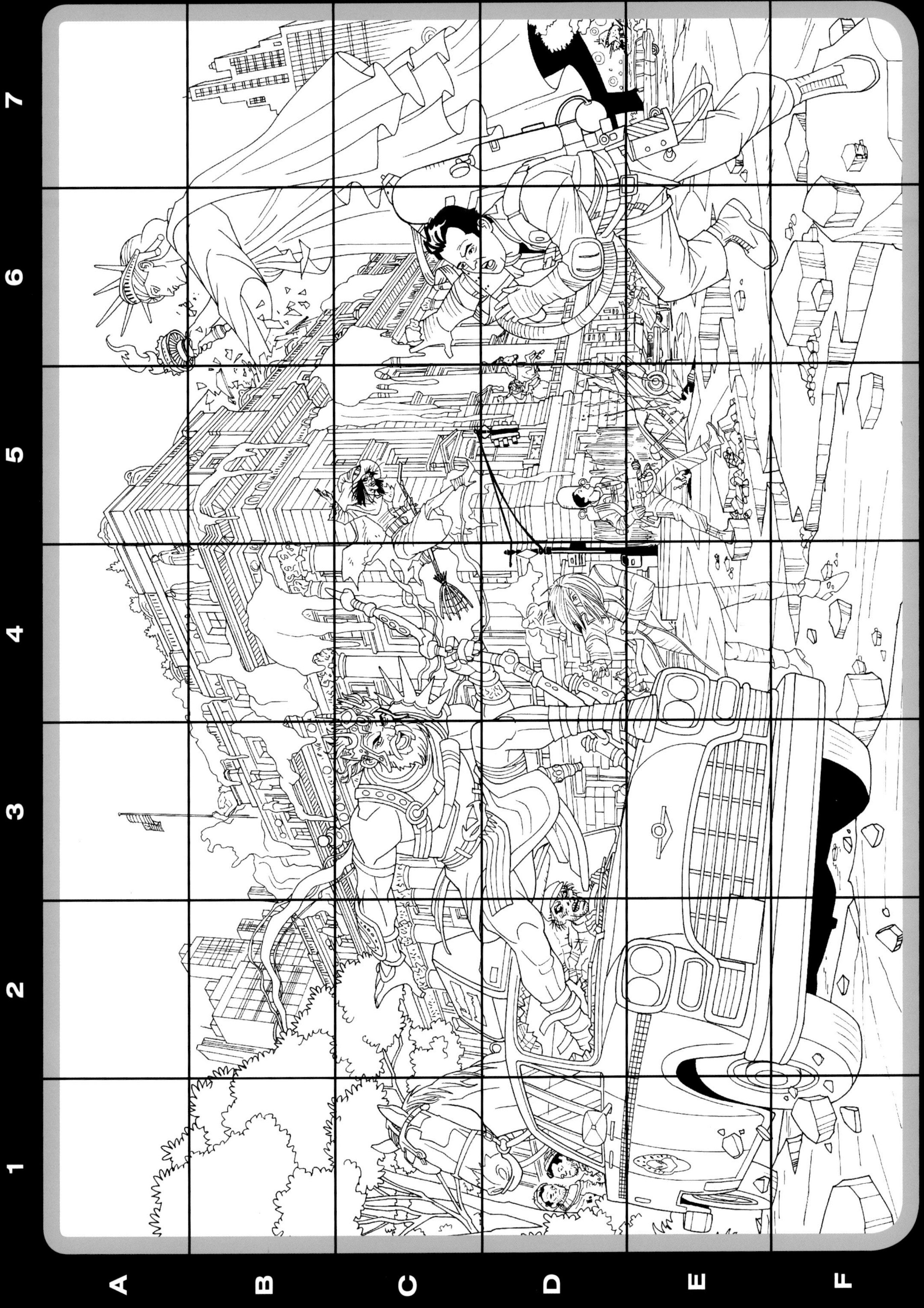
1
2
3
4
5
6
7
A
B
C
D
E
F

VENGEANCE ON VIGO

NERD ALERT
FIVE CONTINUITY ERRORS

1. C6. Winston should be spraying slime, not firing a proton beam.

2. E1. Janosz is in the wrong place – he was lying much further away.

3. D4. The baby should not be lying on the altar! He had been given to Dana to hold by now.

4. D4. The painting of the team should not be in the background. It only appears after Vigo is beaten.

5. E3. The mobile stairs were not beside the painting at this point.

MOVIE MIX-UPS
Items from Ghostbusters

6. F7. The popping eggs are from Dana's apartment, a focal point of supernatural events.

7. E6. This is the takeaway the boys eat to celebrate their first customer.

8. E6. This trolley is from the Sedgewick Hotel – Slimer greedily feasts from it.

9. E2. Repent! This sign was brought to the big showdown with Gozer by a doomsayer.

10. E4. The altar shown here is the one from the roof of Dana's building.

MYTHS AND
MANIFESTATIONS

11. C5. A Chinese dragon – a little snakier and more colorful than its Western cousin. It can bring you good luck – or flash-fry you!

12. D7. Mary, Queen of Scots had her head chopped off in 1587, and has appeared in many places – mainly Scottish castles – since!

13. C7. Did you spot the siren? In ancient Greek tales, sirens lured sailors onto the rock with their sweet song. We have had to provide our visitor with temporary accommodation...

14. C2. Hel, the Nordic goddess of death, has dropped by to brighten things up.

15. A6. The Wendigo. This skeletal creature, sometimes sporting antlers, lives in the great forests of Canada and dines on human flesh (given the chance).

Super Quibble 4: D1. Did you know the significance of the park ranger in the foreground? True behind-the-scenes buffs will know that he is from a deleted scene in which Ray and Winston investigated a paranormal event at Fort Detmerring. Most of the sequence was never used as it contained few laughs. When you see Ray's horizontal encounter with the female Dream Ghost in the movie's big spook montage, that's a remnant of those scenes. Bonus points if you knew all this!

Super Quibble 5: E3. Maybe you were shocked to see Mr Stay Puft in a TV advert in this scene. This never happened in the movie but according to associate producer Michael Gross (the man who designed the Ghostbusters logo), at one stage there were plans to film a Stay Puft advert and have it appear before or after the Ghostbusters' own TV ad. This would have made the Marshmallow Man a familiar figure before his gigantic appearance at the end. Ultimately, it never happened, so top marks if your blooper-meter reacted to this detail!

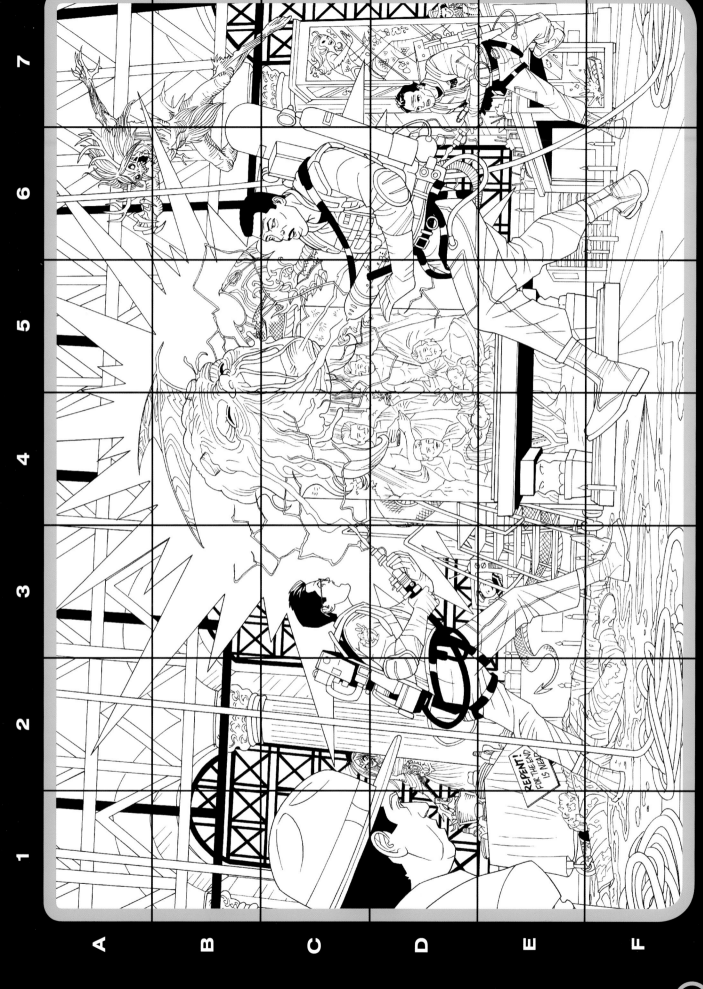

HOW DID YOU DO?

THERE ARE 75 POINTS UP FOR GRABS ON EVERY SPREAD

Check the scoring system on pages 2-3. With eight spreads in the book, your maximum is **600 points**. That's before our 'have we all gone mad?' special offer of **5,551,768 points** (all five Super Quibbles) taking you to the maximum total of **555-2368** – the Ghostbusters' original phone number!

5,552,368: YOU CHEATED! YOU MUST HAVE DONE.
Alternatively, you have a brain the size of Egon's.
Have you thought of collecting spores, molds and fungus?

601-5,552,365: YOU ARE AN HONORARY GHOSTBUSTER.
You know more about the adventures of these guys than they
do themselves. Certainly more than Venkman, anyway.

451-600: IMPRESSIVE. You have a healthy interest in
the Ghostbusters that does not stray into dangerous obsession.
But you should have got more! Still, it's a great excuse
to watch the movies again!

301-450: EXCELLENT. You have the potential to grow
into a useful member of the ectoplasm-blasting community.
Ray would be proud of you. Egon, not so much.

151-300: A GREAT SCORE. You know a lot about the Ghostbusters,
but you probably have a well-balanced life with other,
possibly healthier interests. Winston would salute you!

0-150: GUESS YOU PICKED UP THIS BOOK BY MISTAKE?
But you still tried to get a big score, didn't you? Seems you're
hopelessly competitive and just like doing puzzles. Why not try
your luck with the other *Nerd Searches* in this series, as well?

Published by Hero Collector Books,
a division of Eaglemoss Ltd. 2020
1st Floor, Kensington Village, Avonmore Road
W14 8TS, London, UK.

TM & © 2020 CPII. All Rights Reserved.

Project Concept & Management **Stella Bradley**
Designed by **Paul Montague**

For more books in the series,
order online at **herocollector.com**

10 9 8 7 6 5 4 3 2 1
Printed in China.

ISBN 978-1-85875-856-5